101
WRITING
PROMPTS
FOR HIGH SCHOOL

BOOKS FOR YOUNG WRITERS FROM RED WOLF PRESS:

Mark Trevor's Writing Prompts:
101 Writing Prompts for Grades 3-5 by Mark Trevor
101 Writing Prompts for Middle School by Mark Trevor
101 Writing Prompts for High School by Mark Trevor

Story Starters:
101 Story Starters for Little Kids by Maisy Day
101 Story Starters for Kids by Dena McMurdie
101 Story Starters for Teens by Maisy Day

101 WRITING PROMPTS FOR HIGH SCHOOL

by
Mark Trevor

RED WOLF
PRESS

RED WOLF PRESS

To contact the publisher about permissions, send an email to dmcmurdie@redwolfpress.com.

ISBN: 978-1-955731-09-6

Published by Red Wolf Press.

Interior design and cover design by Dena McMurdie.

Cover art by yusufdemirci, jannystockphoto, and MisterElements.

First printing, May 2024.

IMAGE CREDITS:
Front cover: all images depositphotos—background, hands, pencil, wood grain: yusufdemirci, doodles: MisterElements, post-it note: jannystockphoto.
Back cover: all images depositphotos—woodgrain, plant, pencil, post-it notes, paper clips: yusufdemirci, doodle: MisterElements.
Interior: All images depositphotos. **Page 5:** book: nikiteev, **9:** robot: Leo_Troyanski, **11:** typewriter: kite-kit, **12-21:** speech bubbles: yupiramos, **22-31:** funny happy smiley faces: iliveinoctober, **32-41:** generations concept: yupiramos, **42-51:** hands and notebook: KateBek, **62-71:** shoes and arrows: dashk_ **72-81:** backpacks: CNuisin, **82-91:** graduation caps: cteconsulting, **92-101:** arrows: blue67, **102-112:** hand holding megaphone: Amelisk.

TABLE OF CONTENTS

For Teachers & Parents 6

For Teen Writers 7

Bonus Tips for Aspiring Authors 10

I Wanna Talk About Me 12

This Awkward Moment 22

Keep It in the Family 32

Let's Get Fictional 42

Would You Rather? 52

What Would You Do? 62

Classes, Clashes, and Crushes 72

Oh, the Places You'll Go! 82

What If... ? 92

In My Opinion 102

About the Author 113

FOR TEACHERS & PARENTS

Let's face it—the topics and assignments that high school students often write about aren't particularly interesting or motivating. For that reason, many students don't find writing enjoyable. That's where this book comes in. It contains over 100 writing prompts geared toward today's teens—and their interests!

These pages contain engaging prompts related to friends, relationships, and challenges that pertain specifically to high schoolers. I've also included several fun fiction prompts—something students rarely see in school.

You can use these prompts in various ways: as warm-ups, journal entries, or short pieces that students can expand into longer, more developed essays or stories.

They are also great for narrative, descriptive, informational, and argumentative writing assignments.

My goal in creating this book was to get teens excited about writing—and hopefully turn that enthusiasm into a lifelong passion.

MARK TREVOR

FOR TEEN WRITERS

Writing is challenging and may not come naturally to everyone. However, it is a crucial skill, especially as you look at college, employment, or other endeavors. Many careers require excellent writing skills. Job applications, college admissions essays, and other opportunities depend on your ability to write and communicate effectively.

Here are a few tips to make your writing shine:

1. Stay organized and focused.

Your writing should flow logically and smoothly. Stay focused on your subject, and don't get sidetracked from your main idea. Create an outline highlighting the main points of your essay or story to keep yourself organized and on topic.

2. Support and elaborate on your ideas.

"Show, don't tell" means using details and examples to support your ideas. Instead of simply telling your reader something, offer specific examples demonstrating your point. See the table below for examples of "telling" versus "showing."

Telling:	Showing:
Alisha felt tired.	Alisha was so exhausted that a hundred cups of coffee wouldn't have helped her get to school on time.
My best friend is generous.	My best friend will gladly share her lunch or loan you whatever you need for the prom or a school project.

Continues on the next page.

3. Use strong vocabulary.

Carefully selected verbs and adjectives will bring your writing to life. Here are some examples of how good word choices can improve your sentences.

Weak:	Strong:
The horse ran away.	The boisterous colt dashed out of the corral.
The mountain was tall.	The mountain loomed ominously against the sky.

4. Be concise.

The expression "Less is more" applies to writing, too. Your goal should be to keep your reader's attention while getting your point across. More words (or overwritten sentences) do the opposite. Compare the examples below.

Too wordy:	Clear and concise:
By all accounts, it is believed that the majority of the fish inhabiting the lake had expired.	Most of the fish died.
It was really, really cold, and I just couldn't warm up very much at all.	I couldn't stop shivering.

Tip: Eliminate empty words and phrases, such as: really, just, very, sort of, at all.

5. Remember your audience.

A college admissions essay or letter to an elected official should sound different from a social media post or an informal text to a close friend. Your tone, style, and vocabulary should reflect your audience.

6. Double-check your mechanics.

Poor spelling, sentence structure, or grammar will ruin an otherwise excellent piece of writing. Use free online resources (like spelling and grammar checkers) to look for errors. Reading it aloud will also help you catch obvious mistakes and clunky sentences.

Good writing takes hard work. Your first draft won't be perfect, and that's okay! It needs polishing and editing, and it will improve with each revision.

7. Use AI (Artificial Intelligence) with caution.

AI can be a fantastic tool for writers, particularly for brainstorming or revising a piece of writing. However, using it to create or compose your writing is unethical.

Much AI-generated content is repetitive and can contain inaccuracies.

Teachers, professors, and college admissions people can easily spot an AI-generated essay, and they may penalize you for using it.

BONUS TIPS FOR ASPIRING AUTHORS

Authors often have different motivations behind their writing. For many, it's not fame or fortune but the joy and fulfillment of creating a finished product that others will read and enjoy. Whether you compose poetry, blogs, music, short fiction, scripts, novels, or a memoir, writing is a powerful tool for communicating, inspiring, and entertaining others.

If you are passionate about writing and sharing your thoughts with others, here are some additional things to consider:

1. Read as much as possible.

Reading will increase your vocabulary, improve your grammar and sentence structure, sharpen your mind, and provide effective communication models. It's also an excellent way to examine tropes, pacing, story structure, points of view, character arcs, conflict, style, genres, and more.

2. Write regularly.

Try to write every day, even if it's only in a journal. Don't worry about the length, content, or quality. Get comfortable putting words on paper.

Composing poems, comics, or song lyrics is a fun way to improve your craft. Writing longer works like novels can take months or years, but you can complete an entire book relatively quickly if you devote time to it every day.

3. Edit, edit, and edit some more!

Your writing will improve with each revision. Professional authors know this part of the process is the key to a polished piece of writing. As mentioned earlier, always read it out loud and use online resources (e.g., spell checkers, grammar checkers, or a thesaurus) to make it shine.

BONUS TIPS FOR ASPIRING AUTHORS

4. Join a writer's group or club.

Belonging to a group of dedicated writers (even if it's only you and a couple of friends) will allow you to share your work with others and receive vital feedback and support.

If you don't have a group or can't meet in person, try webinars or find an online writing group. The feedback and encouragement you will receive from other writers is invaluable and necessary before you consider looking for an agent or publisher.

5. Put your work online.

Start a blog, submit to writing sites, or post to platforms like Wattpad, Camp NaNoWriMo, or The Writing Cooperative. This can provide invaluable real-time feedback from readers, writers, and editors. Plus, you could make some money!

6. Never stop learning.

Thousands of books, blogs, videos, and podcasts are available to help writers learn and hone their craft. In addition, abundant resources are available about selling and publishing your work.

Many writers have used the following books to improve their craft, unlock their creativity, or motivate them on their journey.

- *Writing Magic* by Gail Carson Levine
- *Bird by Bird* by Anne Lamott
- *Save the Cat* by Blake Snyder
- *On Writing* by Stephen King
- *The Writing Life* by Annie Dillard
- *On Writing Well* by William Zinsser
- *Story Genius* by Lisa Cron

I WANNA TALK ABOUT ME

Who is your favorite singer or music group?

Why is their music special or important to you? Discuss your favorite songs, lyrics, etc.

_____
_____
_____
_____
_____
_____
_____
_____
_____
_____
_____
_____
_____
_____
_____
_____
_____
_____

I WANNA TALK ABOUT ME

What makes you laugh? Cartoons? Comedies? Dad jokes? Your friends?

Tell us about your sense of humor and what you find funny.

_____

_____

_____

_____

_____

_____

_____

_____

_____

_____

_____

_____

_____

_____

_____

_____

_____

_____

_____

_____

I WANNA TALK ABOUT ME

Where is your favorite place to relax? The mall? The park? The coffee shop? Somewhere else?

Describe why it's your favorite and what you enjoy doing there.

_____

_____

_____

_____

_____

_____

_____

_____

_____

_____

_____

_____

_____

_____

_____

_____

_____

_____

_____

_____

I WANNA TALK ABOUT ME

What makes you angry? Dishonesty? Injustice? Rude or arrogant people?

Discuss two or three things that make your blood boil. Give specific examples.

_____

_____

_____

_____

_____

_____

_____

_____

_____

_____

_____

_____

_____

_____

_____

_____

_____

_____

_____

_____

_____

I WANNA TALK ABOUT ME

Describe your childhood. Was it fun, challenging, or ordinary?
Describe a childhood memory that sticks out above others.

_____

_____

_____

_____

_____

_____

_____

_____

_____

_____

_____

_____

_____

_____

_____

_____

_____

_____

_____

I WANNA TALK ABOUT ME

How do you like to dress?
   Are you about style or comfort?
   What brands or stores are you loyal to?
   Describe what you enjoy wearing and why.

_____

_____

_____

_____

_____

_____

_____

_____

_____

_____

_____

_____

_____

_____

_____

_____

_____

_____

_____

I WANNA TALK ABOUT ME

What is your town or neighborhood like?
   Is it fun or boring?
   What nearby places do you visit regularly?

_____
_____
_____
_____
_____
_____
_____
_____
_____
_____
_____
_____
_____
_____
_____
_____
_____
_____

I WANNA TALK ABOUT ME

What was the best advice anyone ever gave you?

    Who gave it to you?

    Did you follow it?

    What happened as a result?

_____

_____

_____

_____

_____

_____

_____

_____

_____

_____

_____

_____

_____

_____

_____

_____

_____

_____

_____

I WANNA TALK ABOUT ME

What was the most challenging decision you ever had to make?
    What went through your mind?
    How did you feel afterward?

_____
_____
_____
_____
_____
_____
_____
_____
_____
_____
_____
_____
_____
_____
_____
_____
_____
_____
_____
_____

I WANNA TALK ABOUT ME

Are you an introvert or an extrovert? In other words, do you prefer spending time alone or enjoy being around large groups of people? What are the pros and cons of this trait?

_____

_____

_____

_____

_____

_____

_____

_____

_____

_____

_____

_____

_____

_____

_____

_____

_____

_____

_____

THIS AWKWARD MOMENT

Have you ever overheard someone talking about you or one of your friends?

    What did they say?

    How did it make you feel?

    What did you do?

_____

_____

_____

_____

_____

_____

_____

_____

_____

_____

_____

_____

_____

_____

_____

_____

_____

_____

THIS AWKWARD MOMENT

Have you ever shown up at school wearing the same outfit as someone else?

What happened when you saw each other?

What was the rest of the day like?

_____

_____

_____

_____

_____

_____

_____

_____

_____

_____

_____

_____

_____

_____

_____

_____

_____

_____

_____

_____

THIS AWKWARD MOMENT

Have you ever been on a blind date? Who set it up? Write about the date and how it went.

Was it awkward, or did you hit it off?

What did you do on the date?

Did you ever date this person again?

(If you've never been on a blind date, tell about the worst date you ever had.)

_____

_____

_____

_____

_____

_____

_____

_____

_____

_____

_____

_____

_____

_____

_____

_____

_____

_____

_____

_____

THIS AWKWARD MOMENT

Describe an awkward or cringe-worthy situation you witnessed at school.

What happened?

Did you try to record it or take a photo?

Did you tell anyone about what you saw?

_____

_____

_____

_____

_____

_____

_____

_____

_____

_____

_____

_____

_____

_____

_____

_____

_____

_____

_____

_____

_____

THIS AWKWARD MOMENT

Think about the most awkward or embarrassing conversation you have ever had. Who was it with? A teacher? A parent? Your crush?

What was the discussion about?

Did you learn anything from this conversation, or did you try to forget it ever happened?

_____

_____

_____

_____

_____

_____

_____

_____

_____

_____

_____

_____

_____

_____

_____

_____

_____

_____

_____

_____

THIS AWKWARD MOMENT

Think back to your worst "picture day" ever.

What made it so awful? A big zit? Bad hair? A goofy smile? A terrible outfit?

Do you laugh about it now, or does it still make you cringe?

_____

_____

_____

_____

_____

_____

_____

_____

_____

_____

_____

_____

_____

_____

_____

_____

_____

_____

_____

_____

_____

THIS AWKWARD MOMENT

Do your parents post embarrassing photos of you (or themselves) online? Write about a particular picture or post and what happened as a result.

Did your peers see it?

What was their reaction?

What did you say to your parent?

_____

_____

_____

_____

_____

_____

_____

_____

_____

_____

_____

_____

_____

_____

_____

_____

_____

_____

_____

_____

THIS AWKWARD MOMENT

Write about a time when a date or a friend stood you up.

Where were you? A restaurant? A movie theatre? Somewhere else?

How long did you wait for them?

What happened when you saw that person again?

_____

_____

_____

_____

_____

_____

_____

_____

_____

_____

_____

_____

_____

_____

_____

_____

_____

_____

_____

_____

THIS AWKWARD MOMENT

What is the most embarrassing thing that ever happened to you during class?

Did you fall asleep? Pass gas? Get caught picking your nose? Something else?

Describe what happened and how your teacher or classmates reacted.

_____

_____

_____

_____

_____

_____

_____

_____

_____

_____

_____

_____

_____

_____

_____

_____

_____

_____

_____

_____

_____

THIS AWKWARD MOMENT

We all put our foot in our mouths at times. What is the most embarrassing thing you ever said out loud?

   Was it a brainless question or a ridiculous answer? Did you ask or share something private, personal, or insensitive?

   What was the reaction after your poor choice of words?

_____

_____

_____

_____

_____

_____

_____

_____

_____

_____

_____

_____

_____

_____

_____

_____

_____

_____

_____

_____

_____

KEEP IT IN THE FAMILY

Are your parents strict or lenient?

Give an example of something you did (such as skipping school, missing curfew, lying, etc.) and how your parents responded.

_____

_____

_____

_____

_____

_____

_____

_____

_____

_____

_____

_____

_____

_____

_____

_____

_____

_____

_____

_____

KEEP IT IN THE FAMILY

Tell us about your siblings.

How many do you have? How old are they? Where do you fit in? Who do you hang out with the most or the least? Why?

(If you do not have any siblings, write about your cousins or friend group.)

_____

_____

_____

_____

_____

_____

_____

_____

_____

_____

_____

_____

_____

_____

_____

_____

_____

_____

_____

_____

KEEP IT IN THE FAMILY

Everyone's family is different. What makes yours unique?
Which family member is the funniest or most annoying?
Which one, if any, are you most similar to?

_____
_____
_____
_____
_____
_____
_____
_____
_____
_____
_____
_____
_____
_____
_____
_____
_____
_____
_____
_____
_____

KEEP IT IN THE FAMILY

Everyone has pet peeves and sometimes gets annoyed by the people they live with. What are your pet peeves when it comes to your family?

_____
_____
_____
_____
_____
_____
_____
_____
_____
_____
_____
_____
_____
_____
_____
_____
_____
_____
_____

KEEP IT IN THE FAMILY

Write about your grandparents, detailing all you know about them.

When were they born?

What jobs did they have?

Did they serve in the military?

How did they meet?

How many children did they have?

_____

_____

_____

_____

_____

_____

_____

_____

_____

_____

_____

_____

_____

_____

_____

_____

_____

_____

_____

_____

_____

KEEP IT IN THE FAMILY

Describe one of your family's traditions. What makes it so memorable or meaningful to you?

Give specific details about this tradition and why it continues to play a role in your family.

_____

_____

_____

_____

_____

_____

_____

_____

_____

_____

_____

_____

_____

_____

_____

_____

_____

_____

_____

_____

_____

KEEP IT IN THE FAMILY

What is one thing you would change about your family?

Maybe you're an only child or have too many siblings. Perhaps your parents are divorced, work too much, or travel frequently.

Discuss one thing you would change and how it would improve the relationships within your family.

_____

_____

_____

_____

_____

_____

_____

_____

_____

_____

_____

_____

_____

_____

_____

_____

_____

_____

_____

_____

KEEP IT IN THE FAMILY

What does your mom or dad do for a living?

What does their job require? Do they have physical demands or work long hours? Do they travel?

Would you like their job? Why or why not?

_____

_____

_____

_____

_____

_____

_____

_____

_____

_____

_____

_____

_____

_____

_____

_____

_____

_____

_____

KEEP IT IN THE FAMILY

Name a person in your family who you miss the most.

Is it a parent who no longer lives with you? A deceased grandparent? A cousin who lives far away?

Describe what makes this person unique and what you miss about them.

_____

_____

_____

_____

_____

_____

_____

_____

_____

_____

_____

_____

_____

_____

_____

_____

_____

_____

_____

_____

KEEP IT IN THE FAMILY

What is your extended family like?

   Do you have lots of aunts, uncles, and cousins? Where do they live? How often do you see them? How are they different from your nuclear family?

_____

_____

_____

_____

_____

_____

_____

_____

_____

_____

_____

_____

_____

_____

_____

_____

_____

_____

_____

LET'S GET FICTIONAL

Compose a post-apocalyptic story about the last two people on Earth. Who are they? Where do they live? How do they survive?
What challenges do they face, and how do they overcome them? Be descriptive.

LET'S GET FICTIONAL

Write a historical fiction piece about an 18-year-old boy or girl who goes to war. (You can pick any war or time period you wish.)

Why did they go to war? Were they drafted? Did they run away from home?

What happened while they served in the military?

_____

_____

_____

_____

_____

_____

_____

_____

_____

_____

_____

_____

_____

_____

_____

_____

_____

_____

_____

LET'S GET FICTIONAL

Write a story based on a strange handwritten letter you found in your mailbox.

Who is it from?

What does it say?

What action do you take?

_____

_____

_____

_____

_____

_____

_____

_____

_____

_____

_____

_____

_____

_____

_____

_____

_____

_____

_____

LET'S GET FICTIONAL

Compose a creepy story based on this scenario: You become lost while walking in the forest. After a few hours, you see an old house and knock on the door. An old woman answers and says, "Come in. We've been waiting for you."

Do you go inside?

What happens next?

_____

_____

_____

_____

_____

_____

_____

_____

_____

_____

_____

_____

_____

_____

_____

_____

_____

_____

_____

_____

LET'S GET FICTIONAL

You wake up in a large room. It is empty except for two doors. The sign on one door says, "Everything you've always dreamed of... and more." The other says, "You have nothing to lose."

Which door do you choose?

What happens next?

_____

_____

_____

_____

_____

_____

_____

_____

_____

_____

_____

_____

_____

_____

_____

_____

_____

_____

_____

_____

LET'S GET FICTIONAL

Write a story set in the present about two friends with superpowers.

What powers do they have?

Do they use their power wisely or not?

Does anyone know about their powers? If so, what challenges does that create?

_____

_____

_____

_____

_____

_____

_____

_____

_____

_____

_____

_____

_____

_____

_____

_____

_____

_____

_____

_____

LET'S GET FICTIONAL

You wake up one morning, and your house is empty. When you check the date, you learn that ten years have passed, and you are no longer a teenager.

Are you excited or upset about this development?

What happens next?

_____

_____

_____

_____

_____

_____

_____

_____

_____

_____

_____

_____

_____

_____

_____

_____

_____

_____

_____

_____

_____

LET'S GET FICTIONAL

Compose a story using only dialogue between three friends.
Begin your story by identifying the setting and characters. Then, introduce a problem for your characters to solve.

LET'S GET FICTIONAL

You're walking home alone one night when a car pulls up beside you. The driver calls you by name and says, "Get in."

Do you recognize the driver?

Do you get in the car?

What happens next?

_____

_____

_____

_____

_____

_____

_____

_____

_____

_____

_____

_____

_____

_____

_____

_____

_____

_____

_____

LET'S GET FICTIONAL

One afternoon, while hiking in the woods, you discover a cave opening and decide to explore. After a while, you hear strange voices and music coming from somewhere deep inside the cave.

Describe what happens when you descend further into the cave.

WOULD YOU RATHER?

Would you rather spend the weekend relaxing at the beach or hiking in the mountains? Explain why.

_____

_____

_____

_____

_____

_____

_____

_____

_____

_____

_____

_____

_____

_____

_____

_____

_____

_____

_____

_____

_____

_____

WOULD YOU RATHER?

Would you rather fail a class or get cut from the team during tryouts?

    Which one is more humbling?

    How would you cope with this disappointment?

_____

_____

_____

_____

_____

_____

_____

_____

_____

_____

_____

_____

_____

_____

_____

_____

_____

_____

_____

_____

_____

WOULD YOU RATHER?

Would you rather go water skiing or snow skiing? Why did you choose that one?

_____

_____

_____

_____

_____

_____

_____

_____

_____

_____

_____

_____

_____

_____

_____

_____

_____

_____

_____

WOULD YOU RATHER?

Would you rather go to a dance or a sporting event?
Was this an easy choice? Why?

_____

_____

_____

_____

_____

_____

_____

_____

_____

_____

_____

_____

_____

_____

_____

_____

_____

_____

_____

_____

_____

WOULD YOU RATHER?

Would you rather spend the day shopping or in a museum?
Which one is more interesting? Why?

_____
_____
_____
_____
_____
_____
_____
_____
_____
_____
_____
_____
_____
_____
_____
_____
_____
_____
_____

WOULD YOU RATHER?

Would you rather go on a date with your secret crush or see your favorite singer/band in concert?

Which one is harder to turn down? Why?

_____

_____

_____

_____

_____

_____

_____

_____

_____

_____

_____

_____

_____

_____

_____

_____

_____

_____

_____

_____

WOULD YOU RATHER?

Would you rather spend the weekend binge-watching your favorite shows or visiting a water park with your classmates? Why?
Describe which shows you would watch or what rides you would go on with your classmates.

_____

_____

_____

_____

_____

_____

_____

_____

_____

_____

_____

_____

_____

_____

_____

_____

_____

_____

_____

_____

_____

WOULD YOU RATHER?

Would you rather take additional classes or work all summer?
Explain the pros and cons of each option.

_____
_____
_____
_____
_____
_____
_____
_____
_____
_____
_____
_____
_____
_____
_____
_____
_____
_____
_____
_____

WOULD YOU RATHER?

Would you rather have the ability to fly or to read other people's minds?

How would you use these special powers?

_____

_____

_____

_____

_____

_____

_____

_____

_____

_____

_____

_____

_____

_____

_____

_____

_____

_____

_____

_____

_____

WOULD YOU RATHER?

Would you rather spend six months on Mars or in Antarctica? Why?
Describe what you would do and see during that time.

_____

_____

_____

_____

_____

_____

_____

_____

_____

_____

_____

_____

_____

_____

_____

_____

_____

_____

_____

_____

_____

WHAT WOULD YOU DO?

When homeless people start showing up in your neighborhood, do you avoid them or talk to them? Do you try to help them?

Discuss two things your town can do to address homelessness near you.

WHAT WOULD YOU DO?

How do you react when your parents announce that your family is moving to a new town?

What do you say to your friends?

How do you adjust to a new school and town?

_____

_____

_____

_____

_____

_____

_____

_____

_____

_____

_____

_____

_____

_____

_____

_____

_____

WHAT WOULD YOU DO?

Your 16-year-old cousin tells you she "made a big mistake."

What was the mistake?

What is your reaction?

Do you tell anyone about it?

What advice do you give her?

_____

_____

_____

_____

_____

_____

_____

_____

_____

_____

_____

_____

_____

_____

_____

_____

_____

_____

_____

WHAT WOULD YOU DO?

What is your reaction when your parents say you need to get a part-time job?

What type of job do you look for?

What do you do with the money you earn?

WHAT WOULD YOU DO?

Your best friend says they have a crush on your older brother or sister!

How do you react?

Do you try to change their mind?

What problems do you foresee if they start dating?

_____

_____

_____

_____

_____

_____

_____

_____

_____

_____

_____

_____

_____

_____

_____

_____

_____

_____

_____

_____

_____

WHAT WOULD YOU DO?

How would you handle being bullied or harassed on social media? Would you brush it off or fight back?

Who would you tell? Your friends? Your parents? A teacher or counselor?

Describe what you would do in this situation.

_____

_____

_____

_____

_____

_____

_____

_____

_____

_____

_____

_____

_____

_____

_____

_____

_____

_____

_____

_____

WHAT WOULD YOU DO?

For the second time this year, you smell alcohol on your teacher's breath.

Do you ignore it? Tell your parents? Slip a note to the teacher?

Do you think the teacher should lose their job? Explain.

WHAT WOULD YOU DO?

It's Saturday night, and all your friends are attending a party, but you were not invited.

Are you angry? Jealous? Hurt? How do you deal with this?

What do you do while everyone is at the party?

WHAT WOULD YOU DO?

Your house catches fire, and you only have time to grab three things. What things do you take?

Explain why you chose those three things.

WHAT WOULD YOU DO?

Someone gives you a thousand dollars—but with stipulations: You must spend or share it with people you don't know.

Describe two or three things you would do with the money.

_____

_____

_____

_____

_____

_____

_____

_____

_____

_____

_____

_____

_____

_____

_____

_____

_____

_____

_____

_____

_____

_____

CLASSES, CLASHES, AND CRUSHES

Who is your best friend and confidant?

How did you meet this person?

Describe this person's qualities and why you think the two of you get along so well.

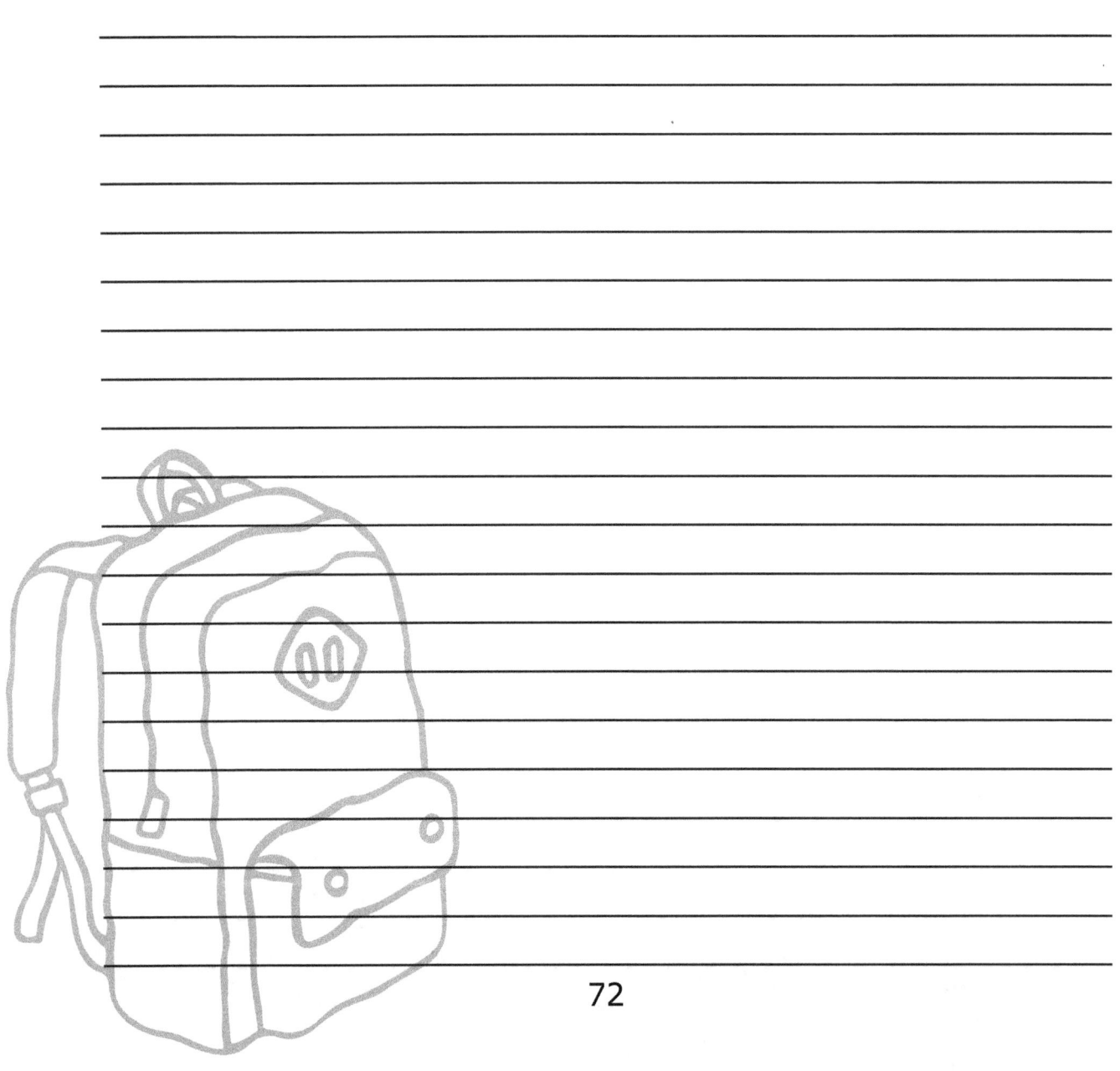

CLASSES, CLASHES, AND CRUSHES

High school is known for its different cliques (e.g., jocks, geeks, stoners, etc.) Name three or four cliques you see in your school.

Which clique, if any, do you belong to?

Do you think cliques are good or bad? Explain.

_____

_____

_____

_____

_____

_____

_____

_____

_____

_____

_____

_____

_____

_____

_____

_____

_____

_____

_____

_____

_____

CLASSES, CLASHES, AND CRUSHES

Imagine you and your best friend have a crush on the same person in your class. How do you deal with this situation?

How does it affect your friendship?

How do you and your friend decide to handle this?

_____

_____

_____

_____

_____

_____

_____

_____

_____

_____

_____

_____

_____

_____

_____

_____

_____

_____

_____

_____

_____

CLASSES, CLASHES, AND CRUSHES

Who is someone in school that you admire? Describe this person and why you might feel this way.

Is it a student or a staff member?

How can you develop those admirable qualities in yourself?

_____

_____

_____

_____

_____

_____

_____

_____

_____

_____

_____

_____

_____

_____

_____

_____

_____

_____

_____

_____

CLASSES, CLASHES, AND CRUSHES

What issues are deal breakers for you in a relationship? Smoking or drinking? Dishonesty? Laziness? Anger issues?

List two to three things you would not tolerate in a relationship and explain why these are so important to you.

CLASSES, CLASHES, AND CRUSHES

Who is the nicest person at your school?
  What makes this person so kind and thoughtful?
  Give examples of what they have done for you or others.

_____
_____
_____
_____
_____
_____
_____
_____
_____
_____
_____
_____
_____
_____
_____
_____
_____
_____
_____
_____

CLASSES, CLASHES, AND CRUSHES

Have you ever had a relationship turn sour? What happened?
Was it a platonic, familial, or romantic relationship?
Did you try to repair the relationship or just move on?

_____

_____

_____

_____

_____

_____

_____

_____

_____

_____

_____

_____

_____

_____

_____

_____

_____

_____

_____

_____

_____

CLASSES, CLASHES, AND CRUSHES

Some relationships are healthy; some are not. What are the characteristics of a healthy relationship and, conversely, the elements of a toxic relationship?

How can you recognize red flags and know when to move on from an unhealthy relationship?

_____

_____

_____

_____

_____

_____

_____

_____

_____

_____

_____

_____

_____

_____

_____

_____

_____

_____

_____

_____

_____

CLASSES, CLASHES, AND CRUSHES

Describe your best (or worst) day ever at school. Who or what made it this way?

CLASSES, CLASHES, AND CRUSHES

Who at school is your rival or nemesis? (No names required.)

Why did you clash?

Describe how this conflict played out. Was it ever resolved?

_____

_____

_____

_____

_____

_____

_____

_____

_____

_____

_____

_____

_____

_____

_____

_____

_____

_____

_____

_____

OH, THE PLACES YOU'LL GO!

What do you plan to do after high school? Do you want to attend college? Do you plan on starting work? Something else?

If college is your intention, what schools or majors do you have in mind?

If you plan on working, what type of jobs are you considering?

_____

_____

_____

_____

_____

_____

_____

_____

_____

_____

_____

_____

_____

_____

_____

_____

_____

_____

_____

_____

_____

OH, THE PLACES YOU'LL GO!

Where do you see yourself living in the future?

   Would you like to stay close to home or move to a different area?

   Explain why you prefer that place. What are the advantages of staying or moving?

_____

_____

_____

_____

_____

_____

_____

_____

_____

_____

_____

_____

_____

_____

_____

_____

_____

_____

_____

_____

OH, THE PLACES YOU'LL GO!

You have been saving money for several months, maybe even years. It's finally time to buy that item you've saved up for. What are you buying? A car? A guitar? A new wardrobe? Something else?

Describe how much you have saved and the item you want to purchase. Why are you buying it? What purpose will it serve?

_____

_____

_____

_____

_____

_____

_____

_____

_____

_____

_____

_____

_____

_____

_____

_____

_____

_____

_____

_____

OH, THE PLACES YOU'LL GO!

Name the one thing you most look forward to as you grow up. Is it owning a home? Getting married? Starting a family? Having a successful career?

Which one is your top priority? Why?

_____

_____

_____

_____

_____

_____

_____

_____

_____

_____

_____

_____

_____

_____

_____

_____

_____

_____

_____

OH, THE PLACES YOU'LL GO!

Name one regret you have. Describe the decision or circumstance and how it has affected you.

What have you learned from it?

How can you avoid this regret from happening again?

_____

_____

_____

_____

_____

_____

_____

_____

_____

_____

_____

_____

_____

_____

_____

_____

_____

_____

_____

OH, THE PLACES YOU'LL GO!

Following high school, what things are you most concerned about? Do you worry about having enough money? Finding a suitable partner? Taking care of your parents?

Describe your biggest concerns about becoming an independent adult and how you plan to handle them.

_____

_____

_____

_____

_____

_____

_____

_____

_____

_____

_____

_____

_____

_____

_____

_____

_____

_____

_____

_____

_____

OH, THE PLACES YOU'LL GO!

How large of a family do you hope to have? One or two children?
More? Or do you prefer to be child-free?

What are the pros and cons of having children?

_____

_____

_____

_____

_____

_____

_____

_____

_____

_____

_____

_____

_____

_____

_____

_____

_____

_____

_____

_____

OH, THE PLACES YOU'LL GO!

You will face more challenges and responsibilities following high school. With this in mind, what two or three bad habits should you reduce or eliminate?

What good habits or characteristics will you need to be a successful adult? Explain.

_____

_____

_____

_____

_____

_____

_____

_____

_____

_____

_____

_____

_____

_____

_____

_____

_____

_____

_____

_____

_____

_____

OH, THE PLACES YOU'LL GO!

You want to attend college, but your parents can only afford a two-year community college. What should you do? Work and save money for a four-year college? Take out a loan? Go to community college?

Explain your decision and why you chose that one.

OH, THE PLACES YOU'LL GO!

How do you feel about the future? Are you optimistic or pessimistic?
Why?

    What societal issues are most important to you?

    Do you see yourself positively impacting the world?

    What can you do to make a difference?

_____

_____

_____

_____

_____

_____

_____

_____

_____

_____

_____

_____

_____

_____

_____

_____

_____

_____

_____

_____

WHAT IF... ?

What if you got a tattoo and your parents found out?
Describe how they would react.

_____

_____

_____

_____

_____

_____

_____

_____

_____

_____

_____

_____

_____

_____

_____

_____

_____

_____

_____

_____

_____

WHAT IF... ?

What if you had to spend the next 60 days living alone in a tree-house in your backyard?

Describe what happens during your time living there.

_____

_____

_____

_____

_____

_____

_____

_____

_____

_____

_____

_____

_____

_____

_____

_____

_____

_____

_____

_____

_____

_____

WHAT IF... ?

What if a new kid arrives at school and looks like they could be your twin?

Do you find it humorous or embarrassing?

How do your friends react?

Do you try to make friends with the new student or avoid them at all costs?

_____

_____

_____

_____

_____

_____

_____

_____

_____

_____

_____

_____

_____

_____

_____

_____

_____

_____

_____

_____

_____

WHAT IF... ?

What if you and a friend decide to hide and sleep at the zoo, mall, or school (pick one) for the night, but things don't go as planned?

Describe what mischief you get into and what happens when security shows up.

_____

_____

_____

_____

_____

_____

_____

_____

_____

_____

_____

_____

_____

_____

_____

_____

_____

_____

_____

_____

WHAT IF... ?

What if you go to a sporting event and something embarrassing happens to you—and it gets broadcast on TV?

Describe what happens at the game. Then, describe what happens the next day at school.

WHAT IF... ?

What if your most embarrassing moment went viral? Describe what happens, how people react, and how you deal with it.

How mortified are you?

Do you ever get over it?

_____

_____

_____

_____

_____

_____

_____

_____

_____

_____

_____

_____

_____

_____

_____

_____

_____

_____

_____

_____

_____

_____

WHAT IF... ?

What if you could go anywhere on vacation for two weeks?
Where would you go?
Who would go with you?
What would you do there?

_____
_____
_____
_____
_____
_____
_____
_____
_____
_____
_____
_____
_____
_____
_____
_____
_____
_____
_____
_____
_____
_____
_____

WHAT IF... ?

What if a family of vampires moved in across the street?
    What happens when they invite you over?
    How do you interact with this family?

_____

_____

_____

_____

_____

_____

_____

_____

_____

_____

_____

_____

_____

_____

_____

_____

_____

_____

_____

WHAT IF... ?

What if AI (Artificial Intelligence) becomes sentient, and you can interact with it like another human?
Describe what might happen.

WHAT IF... ?

What if a massive, unstoppable asteroid is heading toward Earth, and you have a week to live?

Describe how you spend your last days.

_____

_____

_____

_____

_____

_____

_____

_____

_____

_____

_____

_____

_____

_____

_____

_____

_____

_____

_____

_____

_____

IN MY OPINION

Should kids under 18 should be allowed to get tattoos?
Explain your viewpoint and the reasons behind your answer.

IN MY OPINION

Should high school kids have a curfew on the weekends? Why or why not? Support your view.

_____

_____

_____

_____

_____

_____

_____

_____

_____

_____

_____

_____

_____

_____

_____

_____

_____

_____

_____

_____

IN MY OPINION

Is it ever okay for parents to look at your phone or internet history? Why do you feel this way?

_____

_____

_____

_____

_____

_____

_____

_____

_____

_____

_____

_____

_____

_____

_____

_____

_____

_____

_____

_____

IN MY OPINION

Do you think social media is harmful or helpful?
Give examples to back up your stance.

_____
_____
_____
_____
_____
_____
_____
_____
_____
_____
_____
_____
_____
_____
_____
_____
_____
_____
_____
_____
_____

IN MY OPINION

Are people too obsessed with how they look? What could be the drawbacks of focusing too much on one's appearance?
What characteristics should they concentrate on instead?

_____

_____

_____

_____

_____

_____

_____

_____

_____

_____

_____

_____

_____

_____

_____

_____

_____

_____

_____

_____

_____

IN MY OPINION

Do today's teens face too much pressure and unrealistic expectations?
Explain your answer and back it up with examples or research.

_____

_____

_____

_____

_____

_____

_____

_____

_____

_____

_____

_____

_____

_____

_____

_____

_____

_____

_____

_____

IN MY OPINION

Which country or empire is the greatest to have ever existed? Share why you hold this view and include examples that support your viewpoint.

_____

_____

_____

_____

_____

_____

_____

_____

_____

_____

_____

_____

_____

_____

_____

_____

_____

_____

_____

_____

_____

IN MY OPINION

What is the best music genre ever? Rock? Hip-hop? Country? Classical? Explain why you chose that genre and why it deserves to be labeled "the best."

_____

_____

_____

_____

_____

_____

_____

_____

_____

_____

_____

_____

_____

_____

_____

_____

_____

_____

_____

_____

_____

_____

IN MY OPINION

Is a college degree worth the expense, or is it overpriced and over-rated? Are some majors better than others? Which ones?

Discuss the advantages and disadvantages of pursuing a college degree.

_____

_____

_____

_____

_____

_____

_____

_____

_____

_____

_____

_____

_____

_____

_____

_____

_____

_____

_____

_____

_____

_____

IN MY OPINION

Is lying, cheating, or withholding the truth ever okay?
Give examples to support your view.

_____
_____
_____
_____
_____
_____
_____
_____
_____
_____
_____
_____
_____
_____
_____
_____
_____
_____
_____
_____
_____

IN MY OPINION

Should high schools have a dress code, or should teens be allowed to wear what they like?

Explain why a dress code at school is a good or bad idea.

_____

_____

_____

_____

_____

_____

_____

_____

_____

_____

_____

_____

_____

_____

_____

_____

_____

_____

_____

_____

_____

ABOUT THE AUTHOR

MARK TREVOR has been a Language Arts teacher for nearly 25 years and has taught students from kindergarten through grade 12. He currently lives in Cary, North Carolina.

www.ingramcontent.com/pod-product-compliance
Lightning Source LLC
Chambersburg PA
CBHW081002120626
46546CB00010B/2999